T0210004

Christian Princess Diary

Of Confessions

WestBow Press books may be ordered through booksellers or by contacting:

WestBow Press
A Division of Thomas Nelson & Zondervan
1663 Liberty Drive
Bloomington, IN 47403
www.westbowpress.com
844-714-3454

ISBN: 978-1-6642-1728-7 (sc)
ISBN: 978-1-6642-1729-4 (e)

Library of Congress Control Number: 2020925416

Print information available on the last page.

WestBow Press rev. date: 06/14/2021

WESTBOW
PRESS®
A DIVISION OF THOMAS NELSON
& ZONDERVAN

Christian Princess Diary

Of Confessions

Iletha M. Dodds Riggins

This book is dedicated to all my wonderful
nieces and my little King Devan.

A word to the princesses both big and small: Understand that no matter who you are or where you are in your journey, you remain precious in God's eyes. God loves you just as he loves his son Jesus.

Mirror Mirror

On the Wall
Who is the most lovely?

Daily Confession:
<u>I am lovely in the eyesight of God.</u>

Taken from Song of Solomon 5:16

You may not feel beautiful some days but always remember God looks at you daily and you are lovely in his eyes. Write down what you think is lovely.

_____

_____

_____

_____

_____

Mirror Mirror

On the Wall
Who is the most loved?

Daily Confession:

I am God's beloved child.
God loves me and is pleased with me.

Taken from Matthew 3:17

Write down names of people you love including yourself. Do you think God wants you to love people who are sometime mean to you? Why or why not?

_____

_____

_____

_____

_____

_____

_____

_____

_____

Mirror Mirror

On the Wall
Who is the most forgiven?

Daily Confession:

All of my sins have been forgiven.

Taken from Ephesians 1:7

Jesus forgave you of all your sins. Is there someone in your family, school or neighborhood you should forgive? Why or why not?

_____

_____

_____

_____

_____

_____

Mirror Mirror

On the Wall
Who is the most favored?

Daily Confession:

I freely receive God's favor in my life today.

Taken from Ephesians 1:6 HCSB

God's favor is his goodness to us even when we don't deserve it. Do you remember a time someone showed you favor? Do you remember a time you showed favor to someone? Write down what you remember.

_____

_____

_____

_____

Mirror Mirror

On the Wall
Who is like Jesus?

Daily Confession:

<u>As Jesus is in the world, so am I</u>

Taken from 1 John 4:17

Make a list of ways you are like Jesus. How can you be more like Jesus? Take time to study the life of Jesus and as you get to know him you will become more like him.

_____

_____

_____

_____

_____

Little Princess Prayer to invite Jesus in your heart and become more like him

Dear Jesus I ask you now to come into my heart and be the Lord of my life. I pray to become more like you. Jesus please teach me your ways and help me to grow in grace every day.

Amen!

Vocabulary Words

Lovely: having a beauty that appeals to the heart or mind as well as to the eye, as a person or a face. Object of affection or desire.

Beloved: greatly loved; dear to the heart.

Sin: to offend against a principle, standard, etc.

Forgiven: to pardon an offense or an offender.

Favored: excessive kindness or unfair partiality; preferential treatment.

Diary: a daily record of personal activities, reflections, or feelings.

Confession: acknowledgment; avowal; admission.

Forgiveness: the act of forgiving.

Printed in the United States
by Baker & Taylor Publisher Services